THE korean lifestyle book

First published in Great Britain in 2020 by
Michael O'Mara Books Limited
9 Lion Yard
Tremadoc Road
London SW4 7NQ

A CIP catalogue record for this book is available from the British Library.

Papers used by Michael O'Mara Books Limited are natural, recyclable products made from wood grown in sustainable forests. The manufacturing processes conform to the environmental regulations of the country of origin.

ISBN: 978-1-78929-246-6 in paperback print format
ISBN: 978-1-78929-247-3 in ebook format

1 2 3 4 5 6 7 8 9 10

Designed and typeset by Natasha Le Coultre and Barbara Ward
Cover photography: (top) Byeongcheol Jo / Shutterstock, (bottom) IrenaV / Shutterstock, (front flap) Runstudio / The Image Bank / Getty Images
Background images: Shutterstock
Jacket design: Natasha Le Coultre

Printed and bound in China

www.mombooks.com

THE
korean
lifestyle
book

한국스타일

How to Bring K-Culture into your Everyday Life, Home and Style

FOREWORD BY **RYU JEONG HWA**

Michael O'Mara Books Limited

한국스타일

contents

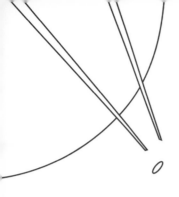

As a Korean, where should I start introducing Korea?

The first time I made a foreign friend was ten years ago, when I went to New York for language training. At the weekend, I would go to watch musicals with six or seven friends of different nationalities. Afterwards, we visited restaurants that served the food of our home countries and ate together, talking about each person's culture. When we went to a Korean restaurant, I gave a lengthy explanation of Korean food, with its flavours of red pepper and garlic, and the all-important kimchi. 'Don't cry because it is very spicy!' I said, jokingly.

Unexpectedly, it was my friend from Mexico who enjoyed it the most. He was of course familiar with chilli sauce and smoky, spicy flavours. He said, 'This isn't spicy enough!' My Japanese and Taiwanese friends, who I thought would have similar tastes to mine, were drinking water, shouting, 'It's too spicy!'

In Korea, it's traditional for people to sit around the table sharing food, such as stew or Korean pancakes, which are served in a large bowl in the middle, alongside several side dishes and often sauce as well. However, some of my international friends were shy about putting their own chopsticks or forks into these communal dishes. It was a totally different point of view from what I was used to, and it was fascinating for me to see Korean customs through their eyes. Some friends were interested in the things I had never thought about, and

foreword

some were unfamiliar with the things I was accustomed to. This is the freshness that interacting with different cultures brings.

In many ways, Korean culture now is very modern and vibrant. But it is still influenced by the old traditions, and sometimes in surprising ways. Hanbok is traditional formal Korean attire, though when lots of us think about it these days we see it as being old-fashioned or a bit boring. It's definitely not that common in Korea any more. But recently we have seen a trend for modern hanbok, with a modernized fit. One of the fashion influencers responsible for making it popular was Jungkook of BTS. He wore it to the airport and it became a hot topic worldwide. Even Koreans were surprised at his unexpected choice, though it showed that this traditional dress could look unique to those who were unfamiliar with it. As a result, more celebrities and young people began seeing modern hanbok as a fashion item. If you try it on, you will feel comfortable and special.

In the chapter on K-beauty, you can read about another very common thing in Korea that has attracted lots of interest from overseas. Seshin is a traditional method of exfoliation – using a special mitt – that's practised in saunas. So while it doesn't feel like a 'unique skincare method' to me, because everyone in Korea is familiar with it, it is certainly an effective skincare method! Try it, and you'll find your skin becomes smoother and will feel invigorated. In my case, if I don't seshin, after two weeks my whole body becomes itchy.

South Korea has become known around the world by the incredible global success of K-pop bands like BTS, and recently the movie *Parasite*, which was the first ever foreign-language film to win the Oscar for Best Picture, and the first Korean film to win

an Oscar in any category. In the chapter about K-pop, you can read about the beginnings of the genre, with Seo Taiji and Boys in the 1990s. After all, knowing about this will surely help readers to understand more about BTS – BTS's Jin calls Seo Taiji 'father', which speaks for itself! – and K-pop. And once you have read about this, you can delve further into the wonderful world of K-pop via the playlist at the end of the chapter.

Korean dramas are fast becoming popular in some European countries as well as Asia, the Middle East and South America. From romance to political, medical and historical dramas, K-drama tells unique stories using some amazing visuals. I hope you are inspired to brave the subtitles and give it a go, if you haven't already. As Bong Joon-ho, the director of *Parasite*, said in his Golden Globes acceptance speech, 'Once you overcome the one-inch tall barrier of subtitles, you will be introduced to so many more amazing films.'

Koreans have the same issue with the language barrier when we watch European and American shows of course, and I hope you will meet and love Korean dramas just as we Koreans love *Sherlock* and *Black Mirror*.

Most of all, this book includes so many useful tips that you can apply in your everyday life. The first chapter on K-beauty explains the specific steps for great skincare, Korean-style, from double cleansing to toner, essence and sunscreen. It also introduces several products which will allow you to get the much-coveted glass-like look, avoiding heavy, full make-up.

The food chapter introduces special dishes that are central to the way we like to eat. Korean foods are healthy and good for the body and skin, so try them! The chapter on the Korean home was useful even for me! The next time I decorate, I will try painting the ceiling the same colour as the wall and placing a mirror in just the right spot for a wider and more spacious look. You will be an Instagram star following these steps!

I don't know how you came to open this book, how much you know about Korea, and what made you interested in my home country. You may be a fan of K-pop stars, or maybe you enjoyed our hit movies, like *Parasites* or *Train to Busan*, or addictive Korean dramas. Perhaps you became interested in K-beauty because you wondered how Korean actresses manage to keep their skin looking so healthy and radiant. In any case, I think this book is the perfect introduction to the contemporary culture of South Korea.

I'm only exaggerating a little when I say that, after reading this book, if one day you have the chance to meet BTS, they will be surprised at your knowledge of Korea!

Ryu Jeong Hwa

한국 스타일

it all
starts
with
your skin

Glow and bare

SKIN-FIRST PHILOSOPHY

'Invest in your skin, it's going to represent you for a very long time.'

LINDEN TYLER

Whether you are a skintellectual already obsessed with the Korean beauty mantras or don't know your essences from your ampoules, this chapter includes plenty of skincare advice and tips on different products to help you to achieve the much coveted 'glass skin' look.

People everywhere have been inspired by South Korean skin philosophy. The country's skincare industry is an innovative leader, with an intensive knowledge of how we can best look after our skin. Thorough and intricate beauty regimes, and in particular the 10-step skincare methods, are hugely popular in South Korea and around the world, and have been adopted by those seeking crystal-clear skin.

No one is promising miracles, but following the Korean skin-first philosophy will revolutionize your beauty routine and make-up habits. You'll have healthier, glowing skin.

As well as helping you to achieve great skin the K-way, this chapter is packed with all sorts of beauty tips, from how to achieve

피부가

먼저라는

철 학

a range of make-up looks, to advice on the best serum to choose according to your skin type and a guide to picking the right sheet mask. You'll be researching essence and reaching for your magnetic nail polish in no time!

SKIN SAVIOURS: SLEEP AND H$_2$O

K-beauty is not just about extensive and well-devised skincare routines and using hydrating products on your skin; it is also about nourishing your body and keeping yourself hydrated from the inside.

K-beauty experts believe in the holistic method of looking after yourself to promote healthy-looking skin, which means they are big advocates of two major factors: drinking enough water and getting enough sleep.

Water, water and more water

South Koreans understand that staying hydrated by drinking plenty of water helps their skin to look healthy and keeps their complexion smooth. Drinking at least eight glasses a day is a natural habit – many homes even contain water-purifiers that can track how many glasses each family member has drunk each day, to make extra sure no one forgets! And, as well as keeping their water intake high, South Koreans also drink plenty of iced tea, green tea and barley tea. Barley tea is usually drunk after meals as a detoxification drink and, like water, it helps flush out toxins from your body and can help keep your complexion clear.

And rest

Sleep is a major factor in the K-beauty routine because of the benefits that getting a good night's sleep can have for your skin. Rest is an aid to rejuvenation and while you are sleeping your skin repairs itself: blood flow increases, which allows it to rebuild its collagen reserve while also repairing damage caused by pollution and UV exposure. Poor sleep patterns or lack of sleep means you are more likely to suffer from dark and puffy circles under your eyes, and underlying skin conditions won't be given enough chance to heal.

Being in bed by 9.30pm is considered essential by K-beauty experts, with the hours between 9pm and 2am often called 'the golden hours', when you should definitely be sound asleep if you want to achieve a flawless complexion.

'Beautiful skin begins with exceptional skin care.'

TIP

Combine a good night's sleep with a sleeping mask which can deliver a spa-like treatment for your skin, allowing it to absorb a range of nourishing and moisturising ingredients while you slumber.

BARE AND BEAUTIFUL

Central to the Korean way of life is a belief in structure, time and ultimately results – in this case, flawless skin. Nobody believes in quick-fix solutions. Instead, optimum luminosity is achieved by focusing on a consistent routine that includes layers of hydration. Pasting foundation over sad and unhealthy skin is a thing of the past.

TIME TO CHANGE

So the key here is time: it's time to slow down and give your skin the attention it deserves. It's time to focus on the skincare rituals that work, that aren't about speed but necessity. Let's focus on how layering the right skincare products is much more beneficial than quick, all-in-one solutions. Because, let's face it, sometimes we reach for the all-in-one beauty product that seems much quicker to use, or skip a stage in our skincare routines because we don't feel like we have time to focus on ourselves. This is the greatest mistake you can make. The Korean skincare ethos is simple and straightforward: make time to look after your skin. You only have one face, it should be treated with the utmost respect. You'll be rewarded with a beautiful, clear and healthy complexion.

If you're not used to making time for your skin, a 10-step regime might seem excessive, but there really is no excuse not to spend time on it. So let's ask ourselves why we neglect and rush this part of our beauty routines and how we can adopt this Korean skin-first mantra.

'Do you have any hobbies?
Yes, skincare.'

SKINCARE ROUTINE

The daily 10-step skincare routine is the ultimate K-beauty regime. It is adaptable for your morning and evening skincare schedule, and each step and product has its own important part to play in keeping your skin clear, healthy and glowing. There is no miracle to beautiful skin, it's just about daily commitment and layering.

Some beauty experts may recommend an extra couple of steps depending on your complexion needs, and it is becoming increasingly common to practice a stripped-down version where clever new products replace multiple steps with just one. But when it comes to high standards of skincare, the 10-step routine is still regarded as the one to follow.

Within the advised 10 steps, there are three essential ones that form the basis of K-beauty philosophy in action. K-beauty experts recommend that if you really can't complete them all, these are the ones that are vital. First, cleanse with an oil-based cleanser or cleansing milk. Then use an antioxidant ampoule or serum (explained on p20–21) to give your skin a dose of goodness, then moisturise to keep the serum you have just applied and all the moisture in your skin 'sealed in'.

10-step skincare routine

1 The first step of the all-important 'double cleanse' is to use an oil cleanser or cleansing milk to remove make-up and draw out other oil-based impurities, like sun cream. Massage into dry skin in the morning and evening.

2 The second cleanser to use is a water-based cleansing foam which helps dissolve and remove all the water-based impurities that your oil cleanser didn't. Apply the foam to your damp face in the morning and evening and massage in a circular motion before rinsing with warm water.

3 Exfoliate your skin using a chemical exfoliator to clean your pores and remove dead skin cells. This step needs to be done once a week and will help your skin absorb other products as well as allowing them to work more efficiently (see *Chemical exfoliators explained* on p22).

4 Apply a thin layer of toner to remove any leftover residue from your cleansers. The toner will also repair your skin's barrier to help it effectively absorb the other products you are about to apply as well as balancing moisture and the skin's pH levels.

5 Apply essence, which is a concentrated formula that targets wrinkles, uneven skin tones and will help maintain a youthful appearance. Think of this as the hydrating layer that primes the skin to best absorb your serums and cream that follows.

6 Ampoules, which are similar to a serum but more like a supercharged one, should be applied next. They comprise a higher amount of active ingredients to target specific skin concerns and usually come in a small glass bottle with a dropper.

7 But don't ditch the serum altogether – this is the next step. Serum targets areas that need extra attention, like wrinkles, dark spots and dehydrated areas (see *Serious about serums* on p24).

8 Smooth eye cream across both your brow and socket bone, moving from the inner to the outer part of your eye. This is the most delicate and thin area of skin and it's important to keep this area protected and hydrated all day long.

9 Moisturizer should be applied as a light layer across your face, but it's important to pick the right one for your skin type. There are so many types of moisturizer all targeting specific skin concerns that finding the right one for your complexion can be tricky (see *Making your moisturizer work for you* on p26).

10 Sun cream time! While some moisturizers already include UV protection, applying a separate sun screen as the last part of your morning routine will help protect your skin against the development of fine lines and wrinkles.

TIP

Vogue has noted a new trend sweeping K-beauty known as the 'skip-care' routine, which uses multitasking products to effectively consolidate the 10-step routine. The thinking is that you aren't cheating, but making your beauty routine more sustainable by cutting out the number of packages required – the mantra behind the 10-step philosophy still holds firm as you aren't skimping on a 'step', but rather combining two steps in one product. For example, look for products that reduce the need for a double cleanse or a toner that works as a hydrating essence as well.

CHEMICAL EXFOLIATORS EXPLAINED

Salicylic acid, lactic acid and glycolic acid might sound like severe ingredients but these chemical exfoliators are the key to clean and clear skin. The Korean skincare philosophy has no time for physical exfoliators that are harsh and damaging to the skin and instead promotes the benefits of chemical exfoliants, which work by safely removing the top layer of dead skin to allow new, healthy skin to show through.

There are lots of different chemical exfoliators on offer; it all depends on your skin type. Below is a list of ingredients to look for when picking an exfoliator, so you can figure out what's right for you. Your skin will thank you for knowing your acids!

ACID INDEX

AHA (alpha-hydroxy acids) are water-soluble and the ones you go for if you need to brighten your complexion. AHAs are great chemical exfoliants because they will improve your skin-cell turnover for a clearer, brighter appearance.

Types of AHA:

Glycolic acid. This acid can improve the skin's appearance by offering a deep exfoliation. It will also help improve uneven skin tone, dark spots and reduce fine lines.

Lactic acid. More gentle than glycolic acid, this acid will help exfoliate and encourage cell renewal. This is a good multitasker acid and is as hydrating as it is exfoliating.

Mandelic acid. This contains larger molecules than other AHAs, which makes it more gentle but no less effective on your skin, leaving it brighter and stronger.

BHA (beta-hydroxy acids) are oil-soluble and able to penetrate deeper into your pores to dissolve excess sebum that mixes with dirt and bacteria to cause spots.

Types of BHA:

Salicylic acid. This is acne's worst nightmare because of its anti-inflammatory and anti-bacterial qualities. It will help calm and clarify the skin and reduce the number of blocked pores.

PHA (poly-hydroxy acids) are relatively new on the skincare scene but offer quite a gentle chemical exfoliant. Often used by K-beauty consultants as an alternative to AHAs, they offer a more soothing skin penetration to both AHAs and BHAs with a gentler exfoliating action. But don't mistake their gentleness for ineffectiveness; they are ideal for all skin types – normal, dry, combination, oily – and while spot-prone skin might benefit from the additional use of salicylic acid for a deeper pore clean, PHAs will still exfoliate soothingly and commendably.

Types of PHA:

Gluconolactone. A powerful antioxidant that helps protect the skin from UV damage by helping strengthen the natural barrier functions. It also helps ensure healthy hydration levels within the skin.

Lactobionic acid. Promotes firmness within the skin and helps tackle signs of ageing and enlarged pores.

SERIOUS ABOUT SERUMS

There are so many serums on offer that choosing the right one for your skin is crucial if you want to reap the benefits of using it as part of your 10-step skincare routine.

Spot-prone skin: look for salicylic acid, which unclogs pores; zinc, which can soothe irritation; retinol, which reduces inflammation; and vitamin C, which increases collagen production, will even out skin tone and enhances your skin's repair process.

Dry skin: look for glycolic acid, which helps discolouration and gently exfoliates; vitamin E, an antioxidant, which can help protect skin cells from damage; and hyaluronic acid, which retains moisture.

Dull-looking skin: look for green tea extracts, which promote healing, hyaluronic acid and vitamin C.

Wrinkle-prone skin: look for retinol, a vitamin A derivative. Retinol is the ultimate ingredient to help tackle fine lines and wrinkles.

MAKING YOUR MOISTURIZER WORK FOR YOU

As the crucial penultimate step in your 10-step K-beauty routine, a light layer of moisturizer on your face will help seal in all the goodness from your previously applied toner, essence and serum. But what moisturizer should you use?

As a general rule, moisturizers incorporate ingredients that fall into four categories: humectants, emollients, occlusive and ceramides. Which of these is the most important for you, and so should be the dominant ingredient in your moisturizer, will depend on the job you need your cream to do.

Humectant-based moisturizers: Often gel-like formulas with a lightweight consistency, these are good for oily skin and are absorbed very quickly. Hyaluronic acid is a powerful humectant, and can help you to get that dewy glow.

Emollient-based moisturizers: These are more creamy or light lotion formulas and are known as 'space fillers', filling in the cracks on your skin and helping smooth out its surface. They are good for normal, dry or combination skin types.

Occlusive-based moisturizers: These are generally best for mature or dry and dehydrated skin. They tend to be thicker in consistency and block the evaporation of water from your skin by forming a film on the top layer.

Ceramide-based moisturizers: Ceramides are produced naturally in the body and are found in high concentrations in the uppermost layers of skin. Ceramide-based creams penetrate the skin easily and help seal in moisture, strengthening your skin barrier. They are good for dry skin or skin that is sensitive and prone to irritation.

수분크림

TIP

Be skintellectual. Finding out what works for you and your skin isn't always easy, so be prepared to research and ask for free sample products where possible and also be flexible. What works well for your skin now might not in the next year or so.

Come up with a list of your main skin concerns and work out which ingredients are most likely to help. You can then start to research the best products containing those ingredients that fit your budget. Don't get caught up with whether it's an essence or a serum; look at the ingredients and see whether there is a high concentration of what you require.

DOS AND DON'TS OF SKINCARE ROUTINES

Don't ever rush or skip a step of your skincare routine. Your skin will not forgive you.

O

Do your research. Where possible, use trial and error and make sure you are wholly satisfied with each product you buy. There should be no buying for the sake of it.

Do keep a beauty diary and record how your skin reacts to different products over time. It's a good way of seeing which items are working so you can ditch the ones that aren't.

○

Do use your ring finger to apply your eye cream every morning and night. This gentle touch is especially recommended for eye-cream application as that finger places the least amount of pressure on the delicate eye area.

○

Don't experiment before a big event. If you want to try out new products, make sure you allow a good time frame to assess results. You don't want to try out a new serum the night before a party you're looking forward to, for example, in case your skin reacts to it and becomes irritated.

○

Do take advantage of every drop of essence in your sheet mask (see p33). When you remove your mask let the excess essence soak into your skin. If you don't have time to let it absorb, use a cotton wool pad and gently massage the essence into your face and neck area so your skin reaps even more benefits.

○

Do always think about the best hydrating products. Layering products that are packed with the most hydrating ingredients means they will penetrate your skin most effectively. You'll be able to see the results – younger-looking skin that glows – sooner rather than later.

Do use mist spray. Keeping a water-based mist spray in your bag is a really simple way of making sure you can give your skin a quick moisture surge throughout the day.

O

Don't forget that skincare products exist on a scale; you can always find a product that is lighter or more water-based than the one you are using.

'One mask, one day'

SESHIN SHINE

A Korean body scrub, or seshin, is a traditional exfoliating skincare ritual in Korea. This pink-skin-inducing deep body scrub is best performed if you can visit a sauna first or have a long bath so that your skin's pores are open. Therapists will use exfoliating mitts to rid your body of dead skin cells, leaving you with skin that has never felt so soft. Lots of spas and beauty parlours offer seshin on their treatment lists but be prepared, the therapists will take every inch of your skin in their scrubbing-mitt hands and give your body a thorough working over! It's intense but it's magical and your skin will literally glow afterwards.

DIY TREATMENTS FOR A HOME SPA TREAT

Scrubs

If you don't want to book into a spa for a seshin treatment, you can perform your own deep body exfoliation at home with the help of some scrubbing mitts, a tub of body scrub and a soak in a hot bath as preparation. Korean beauty therapists use the Korean Italy towel, which is a mitten you can use to remove dead skin cells. Just remember to soak in a hot bath for a least twenty minutes beforehand and then gently scrub away, avoiding your face and other sensitive areas!

Masks

Just because you have a dedicated skin routine it doesn't mean you have to panic if you find yourself running low on an essential. For example, if you run out of sheet masks (see the handy guide on the next page), cotton wool pads covered in the serum of your choice and placed over your face for a few minutes are a great quick way of getting a hydration boost.

Towels

For an effective and simple pore-centred treatment, try putting a warm cotton towel or flannel over your face for five to ten minutes. Put the towel in boiling water, let it cool a little, then squeeze off the excess and put the towel over your face to open blocked pores before splashing your face with cold water to help close and tighten them.

A GUIDE TO SHEET MASKS

Sheet masks form a staple of the Korean skincare routine because of their ease of use and adaptability. They work as a hydrating tool because the cotton-based sheets are infused with serums or essences and the sheet creates a protective barrier on your skin that stops any of the mask's essential ingredients from evaporating. The theory is that they trap the active ingredients on the skin, forcing it to lock in the moisture and reap the benefits. As well as sheet masks for your face, you can get ones for your hands, feet, lips and under-eye area; there are so many possibilities!

Sheet masks can be used for other general skin problems, such as brightening dull complexions, anti-ageing, acne control and for reducing pore size too.

So what sort of mask might be best suited to your skin? An antioxidant **acai berry** mask will leave the skin looking alive and full of elasticity again, perfect for dull complexions that need a 'pick-me-up'. **Aloe** masks work with the same principles of rejuvenating and hydrating your skin, **bamboo water** is ultra-moisturizing, and **bee venom** is good for all types of troubled skin. **Charcoal** masks can detox, exfoliate and draw out impurities such as bacteria or environmental toxins trapped in the skin, while **cucumber** masks can have a cooling, calming effect on hot, irritated skin. **Green tea** masks are moisturizing and calm redness, while a **honey** sheet mask is all about nourishing and soothing with its antibacterial properties. **Pomegranate** sheet masks are good to hydrate and brighten all skin types while **red ginseng** masks are used for the herb's anti-ageing properties. **Snail mucus** extract helps calm irritated skin and leave it thoroughly moisturized while **tea tree**-infused masks will help reduce redness with its anti-inflammatory properties.

MAKE-UP MADE SIMPLE:
THE NO-MAKE-UP MAKE-UP

While there is an attitude of 'more is more' when it comes to following the Korean skin routines, the exact opposite is said when it comes to make-up. The key to Korean cosmetics is understated – subtle yet impactful. It's all about looking like you are not wearing much at all. Think natural yet classic.

Top 10 best K-beauty make-up products to try

1 **Primers:** K-beauty primers are similar to their Western counterparts but with added extras. While the main purpose is to improve the longevity of foundation, there are lots of Korean primers that aim to brighten and colour correct your complexion. They come in shades like pink or lavender to counteract sallowness, as well as containing light-reflecting pigments to give that glass skin look.

2 **BB or CC creams:** Beauty balms or colour correctors are multiple-in-one foundation and skincare products. Depending on which one you choose, they provide either high or low coverage and high SPF sun protection ratings. Many K-beauty make-up experts use them instead of foundation.

3 **Cushions:** Quite a few Korean make-up products now come in a 'cushion compact' which is basically a compact with a sponge bottom layer that is soaked in make-up with an antibacterial applicator sponge on top. Because of the aerating effect of the cushion, the products tend to be light and give a 'dewy' finish.

4 **Concealers:** These differ greatly to foundations and BB creams, which opt for the glowy effect; concealers are all about high coverage and longevity.

5 **Contouring:** This can be done with either cream or powder products depending on your preference, but remember, the look you want to achieve is subtle and natural; you're trying to soften the face rather than going for dark, visible strokes. Opt for light colours without any orange or red undertones and don't forget to work a little along the jawline to soften it and round out the effect.

6 **Highlighters:** Your skin should be glowing from the beginning, so this isn't a big step in most K-beauty bloggers' lists, but if you need a little extra brightness, opt for cream-based highlighters and apply down the bridge of your nose and down the centre of your chin, your cupid's bow and the centre of your forehead, as well as your cheekbones. Just remember to blend it well.

7 **Eyeshadows:** These tend to be subtle and deposit less colour on the eyelid than you would expect. They give a soft finish rather than a heavy, pigmented one. Peaches, pinks and soft browns are the most popular colours for an everyday look.

8 **Eyeliners:** Aside from the classic black, soft neutral tones are the most popular; apply along the top of your lash line and the outside third of the bottom of your lash line and smudge for a natural-looking smoky effect.

9 **Blushes:** Cream blushes give a natural wave of colour and youthful glow and are more popular than powder blush thanks to them maintaining the coveted 'glass skin' effect. Start by applying at the high point of your cheek and blend out and downwards.

10 **Lip tints:** Ultra-hydrating (would we expect anything else?!) and sheer, these lip stains both moisturize and provide a subtle wash of colour. Tinted lip balms are also a must-have in your make-up bag. Choose lip colours that are in the same colour family as your blush for a professional finish.

KOREAN MAKE-UP TRENDS AND ROUTINES

Korean make-up style is, in essence, about making the skin look bright and healthy. Try to find products that can offer you dewy skin, lightly stained lips and soft, shimmering lids, which together produce a classic Korean look.

There is no one set make-up vibe or look and, much like fashion, how you rock your cosmetics is completely based on individual likes and dislikes. You might prefer the no-make-up make-up look or find that you add a dark dash of lip stain and flick your eyeliner for a more impactful, 'daebak' (awesome) Instagram effect.

HOW TO ACHIEVE THE
PERFECT GRADIENT LIP LOOK

The gradient lip effect, the most popular pout in K-beauty, is all about simple preparation and careful application of colour to achieve the subtle and youthful lip look.

Firstly, you need to exfoliate your lips. There is a range of lip exfoliants to choose from. By exfoliating this delicate area of your face you'll be ridding it of dead skin cells, which will help to create a soft and smooth canvas for the lipstick layer. Rub the lip exfoliator in a circular motion gently on your lips for fifteen to twenty seconds before delicately rinsing.

Now pack some moisture back into your lips with a rich lip balm – opt for one that contains shea butter or olive oil as they will help nourish your lips. Leave to dry for a few minutes and then apply a thin layer of concealer. The gradient lips look is all about the contrast of dark and light shades, so using concealer on your lips first will give you a better canvas to work on. Using your finger, apply a small amount of concealer across your lips, making sure the coverage is even and not too thick.

Next put on a lipstick in a colour that works for you, but only apply it to the inner part of your upper and lower lip. Now, using your finger or a cotton bud, blend the edges of your lip colour in a gentle left-to-right motion. You'll probably find that a cotton bud makes it easier to blend more professionally as it can help delicately move colour into the corners of your mouth.

If you like the matte look for your lips then your gradient lip look is complete, but you can also apply a thin layer of clear lip gloss to your pout for a shiny finish. This will give your lips an extra dewy, deliciously sleek look.

립 그라데이션

K 팝과 K 뷰티

K-pop and beauty

In the world of K-pop, make-up is experimental and fun; members of your favourite K-pop group will be happy to try out a range of looks depending on their mood and current style. There are even beauty brands dedicated to products that will give you your favourite K-pop star's look. MTPR teamed up with BTS for their range of coloured contact lenses with each member as 'the face' of a different shaded contact.

Blackpink often share their favourite make-up trends and beauty products on their Instagram alongside their daily beauty 'must-haves'. For example, when Lisa wants to go for a dramatic, smoky-eye look, she knows exactly what to reach for. 'I find it's perfectly acceptable to have no eyeliner but mascara is a must,' she revealed. While Jennie is all about experimenting: 'My style varies on my mood or the weather. I do not stick to one style only and I prefer mixing and matching brands with a sort of casual-meets-cool sentiment. I find a blatantly girly style with no charm boring.'

Opposite: Blackpink's Lisa with natural makeup.

> TIP
>
> Don't be scared to ignore the intended use of a product. Korean beauty make-up artists often talk about how it's more about the 'look' than sticking to the rules. So use your lip tint as a cream blush if that feels right, or use your contouring powder as an eyeshadow – make the make-up work for you!

PERFECT NAILS: CLASSIC OR CREATIVE

Korean beauty focuses on every aspect of our appearance, which means supple soft hands and strong nails are as important as great skincare. But on top of that, nail care can be an art form and a practised skill. Below are just some of the ways you can achieve the ultimate nail look.

Skin-first philosophy

The skin around your nails is the first thing to consider when it comes to nail care, and if you have dry or rough, cracked cuticles, you need to get moisturizing. As well as using a rich hand or nail cream, try to address any problems in this area by applying a serum to the cuticle for a more intense infiltration. A green tea-type serum will moisturize the area without making it sticky; if you aren't going to paint your nails later that day, apply across the whole nail.

Strengthen the nail

Your nails – or rather the visible part called the nail plate – are made up of keratin protein. Using a nail strengthener to protect your nails against the elements can help limit damage and breaking. You will only need to apply a coat once a week.

Nail mask

In the same way you'd treat your face to a rehydrating sheet mask, give your nails some pampering by applying a nail mask. Hand masks are also a great option to give your whole hand an injection of hydration, but with nail masks the focus is more intense. Try a nail mask that contains goat's milk extract, which works on strengthening brittle, weak nails, or masks that contain glycerine, which can help the nail become more flexible and stand up to more wear and tear.

Aurora nail art

One of the most popular K-beauty nail trends of 2020 is the 'aurora nail' look, which is inspired by aurora borealis, the northern lights. Nails are painted with a gel nail polish that creates a colour-shifting, kaleidoscope shimmering effect as your hand moves due to the metallic particles in the polish.

To create this look at home, you'll need some special magnetic gel polish, and a magnetic wand (which can be bought online). Before you start, buff the nail bed to provide the best surface for the polish to adhere to. Now take your bottle of magnetic nail polish and roll the bottle through your palms for a few seconds to spread the fillings throughout the liquid. Apply a first coat to your nails as if you were applying a standard polish. Allow to dry and then paint a second, thicker coat, making sure you don't let the liquid dry or pool.

While each nail is still wet, hold the magnetic wand over your nail (without touching it) for about fifteen to twenty seconds. Repeat each time, making sure you hold the magnetic wand over polish that hasn't had the chance to dry. Hold it in the same place each time for a more uniform look, but for the aurora nail look, wave the wand over your nail to adjust and distribute the shimmer.

Once that second layer is dry – which might take longer than normal as it is slightly thicker – apply a quick-drying topcoat to your nails. This won't affect the shimmering properties of the gel polish but will ensure a longer-lasting mani.

 TIP

If you want an even more unique look, opt for a different metallic shade for each nail or add a jewel on top of some of your nails.

PRODUCTS AND STOCKISTS

The most important thing is to do your research and look at the ingredients that each product contains so you can get the right result for your skin. To get you started, here are some of the Korean brands that K-beauty bloggers love to rave about.

3CE	Hanyul	Mediheal	Sulwhasoo
A'pieu	HERA	Missha M	Tarte
Age 20's	Holika Holika	Moonshot	The Same
Banila Co.	Innisfree	Nature Republic	TheFaceShop
Clio	IOPE	O Hui	Tonymoly
Dr Jart+	It's Skin	Physicians Formula	Too Cool For School
Espoir	Klairs		
Etude House	Laneige	Secret Key	Troiareuke
Foreo	Luna	Skinfood	VT
Glow Recipe	Mamonde		

Wesbites like **Soko Glam** (www.sokoglam.com), **YesStyle** (www.yesstyle.com) **Net-a-Porter** (www.net-a-porter.com), **Pure Seoul** (www.pureseoul.co.uk), **Tulsi Beauty Store** (www.tulsibeautystore.com), **Selfridges** (www.selfridges.com) and **Cult Beauty** (www.cultbeauty.co.uk) stock a range of K-beauty products, skincare solutions and make-up and offer worldwide shipping.

There are also some amazing K-beauty subscription boxes available which allow you to try out miniature versions of make-up or skincare.

한국스타일

korean
fashion

How to get the style, the vibe and the attitude of Korea's fashion scene

INDIVIDUAL VIBE

'Style is a way of saying who you are without having to speak.'

RACHEL ZOE

South Korea's fashion identity is eclectic and creative; there is a unique vibe to Korean style, and K-pop stars, actors and models, as well as street-style bloggers, all influence the fashion world thanks to their unrivalled sense of style.

It's all about confidence: you can't pull off an out-there look if it looks like the clothes are wearing you. Koreans own their style; they know they look original, they know they look good and they feel good. It's not just about the clothes, but the attitude and personality too.

Opposite: Seoul Fashion Week Street Fashion, Seoul, South Korea, 2019

개성 있는 스타일

Celebrities have a tangible influence on the fashion world; items spotted on famous idols and actors often sell out, and there are numerous style blogs devoted to cataloguing the on- and off-duty looks of the famous and fashionable.

There are no rules when it comes to Korean fashion: the outfits are put together to ooze effortless style but with incredible thought. Colours, prints, patterns, textures, layers and accessories are all mixed together in an eclectic, individual look. Bona fide chic.

MODERN HANBOK

Hanbok is traditional Korean clothing, often brightly coloured and with clean lines, consisting of jeogori (a long-sleeved, collared, wrap-around blouse or jacket) for both men and women, with chima (a long full skirt) for women and baji (loose trousers) for men. While hanbok is rarely worn by Koreans these days outside of festivals, holidays and formal events, contemporary hanbok-inspired clothing is increasingly popular. These modern interpretations tend to be more wearable for everyday dressing, while still adding a sense of refinement.

Take inspiration from fashionable young Koreans, like Jungkook of BTS, who was spotted in modern hanbok from Korean brand Zijangsa, and look for contemporary clothes inspired by historical clothing from your country or culture.

현대한복

Opposite: (top) traditional hanbok in a contemporary fashion show, (far right) actress Kim Jae-kyung in modern hanbok and (right) Jungkook of BTS in casual hanbok

'Poetic, street, tailored ...
That is our style.'

J KOO

Opposite: Street-style outfit during
Seoul Fashion Week, 2019

KOREAN FASHION: SELF-CONFIDENCE

Social media makes Korean style visible around the world. South Korea has opened up a fashion dialogue with the rest of the globe, and is in turn influenced by instant access to new trends, different looks, unusual fashion and traditional style – available with just a click and a scroll. The ideas and inspiration are limitless, but Korean fashion celebrates one unique force in particular: self-confidence. They own their style with conviction.

WHAT IS KOREAN FASHION?

Known for being expressive and reflecting a sense of individuality, Korean fashion is forever evolving and therefore feels new and exciting yet refined with each season that passes. There is always an eclectic mix of streetwear and finely tailored garments on the runway, all styled together in fresh new ways.

Korean style is: Fashion that creates magic on the human body. You look good, you feel good.

○

Korean style does: Accentuate the strength of your body, and emphasizes the power of your personality.

○

Korean style will: Embrace you into the fashion family which is empowering and continually inspiring.

K-POP AND FASHION

Without a doubt, one of the biggest influences on Korean fashion and style are K-pop groups, which are identified by Lyst, the global fashion search engine, as 'major global fashion influencers'. Their popularity has spread far beyond just music and much further than South Korea; fashion labels are cosying up to the genre's global superstars knowing that they are being watched and followed and tweeted about by millions upon millions of fans.

There are hundreds of Twitter accounts that just post about BTS and their fashion choices. Some accounts are even specific 'BTS airport fashion' accounts, dedicated solely to identifying the clothes that each BTS member wears while travelling. There are also numerous fashion accounts on Instagram and Twitter posting about clothes worn by Blackpink, and many other popular K-pop groups.

When Suga from BTS was spotted wearing a checked shirt from Off-White, designed by American fashion darling Virgil

Abloh, online searches for the shirt went through the roof within hours of the photo appearing.

To understand the juggernaut power of persuasion that K-pop has on fashion, look no further than its love of T-shirts. Mamamoo's Moonbyul wore a 'Jesse Jackson '88' campaign plain white T-shirt with simple lettering in the music video for her song 'In My Room'. There was no political statement here – the T-shirt simply created 'a look' – but before long hundreds of fashion sites saw an increase in orders for the boxy white T-shirt. Korean fashion is influential enough to make almost anything cool, even American political nostalgia.

INDIVIDUAL LOOKS

Pushing boundaries and telling fans that too much is never enough is a theme in most of K-pop's trend-defying fashion choices. The slick, fantastically vibrant music videos are put together to be visually stimulating; the outfits are often the centrepiece for the videos.

The members of BTS, for example, all have individual styles and their fashion appeal is greater because they don't just work one singular boyband 'look'. Personality plays a big part in their appearance – the band is made up of members who each have their own fashion sense that fans can identify with. Emulating the style of their favourite member makes fans feel connected to their idols.

Chanel brand ambassador Jennie from Blackpink oozed style as she helped unveil the brand's spring/summer 2020 collection at the Grand Palais in Paris. And sitting beside her on the front row? *Vogue*'s Editor in Chief Anna Wintour, of course.

'Good clothes are good for you'

IRENEISGOOD

Left: Jennie from Blackpink attends
Paris Fashion Week, France, 2019

Right: G-Dragon at the 2017 Chanel show,
Paris Fashion Week, France.

CLASSIC AND TAILORED
VS INDIVIDUAL AND COLOURFUL

Seoul Fashion Week Executive Director Jung Ku-ho defines Korean fashion and Seoul's fashion scene specifically as a mix of streetwear and luxury. It is 'very much involved with street culture; the city is not really into high-end fashion, but more so into affordable streetwear that is influenced by K-pop stars and K-entertainment.' Korean fashion is fresh and animated which makes it appealing to anyone who uses it to express and reinvent themselves constantly and unapologetically. Western designers see K-pop not just as a place for inspiration, but an area in which to immerse themselves and boost sales.

DETAILS, ACCESSORIES, MOTIFS

The Korean style sensibility is accessible to everyone because of its eclecticism; there is no singular definitive style. The K-pop stars who sit in the front row at catwalk shows at fashion weeks are instrumental in bringing the likes of Balenciaga, Gucci and Balmain to a mainstream Korean audience, but the key to emulating their style is that there is no one look. The way they dress is reflective of their environment, and particularly inspired by Seoul itself, as a young, vibrant city full of colourful and exciting designs made by the local fashion brands.

Korean styling is about the little details. Just as Korean beauty is about taking time for your skin, fashion 'looks' are put together with thought and precision; accessories like shoes, bags, glasses and belts can all be used to complete a style.

SEOUL FASHION WEEK

Catching up with London, Paris and New York in terms of its fashion clout, Seoul's streets are ablaze with fashion industry experts, designers, bloggers, influencers and their followers when the bi-annual Seoul Fashion Week (SFW) opens its runways.

SFW has become a global phenomenon since its inception in 2015, thanks to the buzz generated by its new designers, its celebrity appeal and the promise of discovering something different. Park Hwan-sung, designer and creative director of Korean fashion brand D-Antidote notes: 'People here give off a trendy, youthful vibe because designers tend to be younger. Seoul is both modern and contemporary yet with historical aspects and styling is fresh and new.'

K-pop idols and the stars of K-dramas appear next to models on the catwalk or lining the FROW, showcasing the latest looks. From Blackpink's Jennie at Chanel and EXO's Kai at Gucci to G-Dragon at We11Done and Taeyang at Juun.J, you're just as likely to spot a Korean celebrity on the front row of a huge global heritage brand's show as that of a home-grown Korean label.

BTS AND BLACKPINK: LOOKS AND LABELS

Each band member of BTS and Blackpink works a different look and sets a standard for style around the world. Here's a quick glance at the looks and labels that each member of two of the most well-known K-pop bands showcase.

방탄소년단

BTS

RM: Comfy, nature-inspired,
neutral colours, fan of VISVIM

Jin: Classic, clean-cut, simple, loves
pink, fan of Thom Browne

SUGA: Minimalist, oversized, monochrome,
loves beanies, fan of Fear of God

j-hope: Street style, '90s, bright colours,
bold patterns, fan of Supreme and Off-White

Jimin: Chic, elegant, cool, loves skinny jeans
and Chelsea boots, fan of Chanel

V: Experimental, high fashion, arty, loves loose
trousers and flowing shirts, fan of Gucci

Jungkook: Cool, practical, relaxed, loves plain T-shirts
and big stompy boots, fan of Carhartt

블랙핑크

BLACKPINK

Jisoo: Feminine, girly styles, lots of lace
and bows in pastel colours, fan of Burberry

Jennie: Edgy and chic, likes to mix
streetwear with luxury labels, fan of Chanel

Rosé: Prints, florals, monochrome, casual,
relatable style, fan of Yves Saint Laurent

Lisa: Classic high street, loves cargo pants,
caps and crop tops, fan of Celine

'Seoul is attracting the world's attention these days'

MUNSOO KWON

STEPPING OUT IN K-DRAMA STYLE

Footwear giants Yoox and Superga have seized upon the 'couple look' made famous by stars in K-drama shows who often step out in matching outfits as a way of showing their affection for one another. With the trend catching on, the new Yoox and Superga Couple Shoe Range features ten different designs.

K-FASHION STYLE AND MOOD

Korean style and fashion bloggers often select their outfits purely by their mood or a daily mantra. Their look for the day could be created from an inspiring quote or a simple morning affirmation. For example, if you feel like the world is against you, put on your brightest tracksuit, accessorize with bright white trainers and vibrant jewellery and show the world you're ready for a fight! As much as it's about how you look, K-fashion emphasizes how clothes can change your mood, how they are the tools that can brighten or shift your perspective on the day.

DESIGNERS: WHERE TO FIND THE TRENDS

Designer **Goen Jong** of Goen.J offers polished and refined chic.

@goenjofficial

Cres. E Dim. creates seriously cool street-style pieces that combine 'loud' and 'soft' statement pieces.

@cresedim

Irene Kim wants her label to empower people to 'stay true to oneself and embrace one's individuality' and is always bang on the latest trends.

@ireneisgood and @ireneisgoodlabel

KYE (kye-official.com) offers a mix of bold, edgy yet glam pieces. They are available at retailers around the world, including Urban Outfitters.

Juun.J is high fashion with a price tag to match, but follow them on Instagram for cooler-than-cool outfit inspo.

@juun.j_official

YesStyle (yesstyle.com) is good for fun accessories and jewellery, as well as a wealth of skincare and make-up.

Somethin' Sweet (sthsweet.com) stocks affordable fashion and ships worldwide.

TOP SEVEN KOREAN DESIGNERS TO WATCH

Kimmy J

There is something for everyone with this designer: streetwear is combined with classic, tailored designs and every style is wearable and packed with attitude. The air of unpredictability in colours and texture is why it's a firm favourite in Seoul.

@kimmyj_official

MOHO

Derived from the Korean word *moho-hada*, which means ambiguous, MOHO's designer and founder Lee Kyu-ho's creations are a mixture of art and fashion. The aesthetics are sharp but simple; Lee took inspiration for one of his clothing lines from his military service, creating utilitarian yet edgy designs.

@mohocompany

SJYP

Denim designs are central to this streetwear brand, which mixes timeless classics with on-trend pieces. The duo designers behind the brand like to play with patched jackets, distressed skirts and two-tone shorts in a look that pays homage to the nineties' love of denim.

@SJYP.kr / @shopbop

Nohant

This unisex label filters a French nonchalance into its designs, making it casual and not too 'showy'. It also appeals to the younger generation with block colour pieces and bold prints for tees, shorts and sweatshirts.

@official_nohant

KUHO

The focus is on workwear that is experimental and plays with colour and design, and can be transformed from office wear to going-out chic in one easy move.

@kuho_official

J KOO

Mixing sharp tailoring, feminine looks and streetwear culture all in one, the brand is always evolving and developing its aesthetic. Romantic yet sporty looks are a big favourite.

@jkoo_official

M Playground

Found in the trendy Hongdae district in Seoul, M Playground is a brand that is both playful, hip and affordable. Mixing cultural vibes with a stylish edge, the clothes are fashionable and accessible.

@mplayground_official

한국스타일

k-pop

Listen, watch and be entertained: the secret of K-pop

'K-pop is bigger than just one band or icon ... it's a phenomenal juggernaut of musical mastery.'

There are so many K-pop bands and solo stars that have appeared and evolved over the years that it is impossible to pin down the most influential or the ones who are going to go the distance. But if you only focus on one band or artist, you are sort of missing the point of the music.

Opposite top: BTS performing at the 2019 Bilboard Music Awards, Las Vegas, USA

Opposite bottom: Sunmi performs her single 'Lalalay', Seoul, South Korea, 2019

K-POP: WHAT IT IS AND WHAT IT IS <u>NOT</u>

K-pop isn't just about having one favourite band
or idol – it's an ever-changing introduction
to new personalities and new songs.

o

K-pop is bigger than just one band – it's an all-singing,
all-dancing, polished, perfected, cheeky, fun, catchy,
repeatable and iconic phenomenon.

o

K-pop isn't afraid to mix musical genres or
confront difficult subjects.

o

K-pop isn't afraid to not conform – the lyrics don't need
to be translated into English to increase a song's appeal.

o

K-pop isn't tacky or cheap; it's experimental and slick.

o

K-pop is the song you download and can't stop
humming; the music video you stream that blows your
mind; or the performance you watch that makes you
want to learn every single dance move. That is K-pop.

TRADITIONAL KOREAN MUSIC

Before K-pop, the music scene in South Korea was largely slow ballads or 'trot', a fusion of traditional music with a slightly upbeat edge. Traditional music would feature pansori, a style of Korean storytelling set to music played on instruments including the piri (a bamboo flute), kkwaenggwari (a brass gong), janggu (traditional drum) and gayageum (a traditional stringed instrument).

K-pop artists sometimes incorporate traditional Korean music and influences into their songs as a nod to their culture. Monsta X used the taepyeongso, a traditional Korean wind instrument, in the intro to their hit, 'Follow'. G-Dragon blends traditional Korean folk music and American hip-hop into his hit, 'Niliria', a collaboration with American hip-hop artist Missy Elliot. 'IDOL' by BTS also features traditional instruments and elements of pansori – you can hear it in the rhythm and the use of drums, cymbals and the kkwaenggwari gong.

K-POP: THE BEGINNING

In the 1990s, Korea's younger generation were being exposed to American popular culture thanks to the liberalization of the media and developments in communication and technology. At the same time, there was a growing desire to see a fresh, more exciting form of entertainment than the ballads and trot music currently on offer in Korea. Then, on 11 April 1992, musical historians agree K-pop was born, on a TV talent show. Enter Seo Taiji and Boys.

Seo Taiji was a well-known rock star in the heavy metal band Sinawe, but when they broke up he changed his musical focus and turned to hip-hop. He recruited two popular and talented dancers, Yang Hyun-suk and Lee Juno, to join him as backup in his newly formed group, Seo Taiji and Boys. But when they took to the stage on that Saturday in April 1992, no one could have predicted the impact their single, 'Nan Arayo' ('I Know'), would have on the future of Korean music. Their song was a mixture of rap, rock, techno and pop with elements of R&B, with lyrics in Korean. 'I Know' represented the first time American-style pop music had been fused with South Korean culture to create a new musical hybrid.

The band went on to have hit after hit and ignited a trend for youthful, dance-orientated, exciting music from performance-focused groups. K-pop was born.

K-POP: THE ADVENTURE BEGINS

Seo Taiji and Boys disbanded in 1996, but they were responsible for transforming South Korea's musical scene and performance landscape. In this period, three big music management studios emerged: SM Entertainment, JYP Entertainment and YG Entertainment. They all wanted to manufacture groups like Seo Taiji and Boys, but even more polished and sleek, and appealing to Korean teens. The first idol group, H.O.T., from SM, appeared on the scene in 1996 and consisted of five boys who sang, danced and looked the part, with lyrics about social issues that Korean youngsters could identify with – such as bullying in schools.

Girl group Girls' Generation, aka SNSD (Sonyeo Sidae), was a band who embodied everything the new style of music was about – high-quality performances and sleek dancing, an extremely polished aesthetic and, under the guidance of SM management, a continual release of hits. Their 2009 song, 'Gee', became the bestselling single in South Korea that year and epitomized everything K-pop is about: it was fun, infectious and memorable, and performed by cute, picture-perfect girls who had trained hard, rehearsed even harder, and given years of their lives to embark on the journey to becoming a pop star.

K-POP: 'GANGNAM STYLE' AND BEYOND

Unless you have been living under a rock, chances are the words 'Gangnam Style' will instantly conjure up images of a highly energetic, catchy and entertaining music video in which a man in black sunglasses jumps about in a set of choreographed, fast-tempo moves. The signature moves – the horse trot and lasso spin – were devised by PSY and his choreographer, and when the music video was released in 2012 it was an instant hit. It quickly became an internet sensation and hit the top of the charts in over 30 countries. 'Gangnam Style' harnessed the power of the internet and made a global star out of an artist rapping in his native Korean.

Whether you class 'Gangnam Style' as a novelty hit or not, there is no denying the path it paved for the future of K-pop. Suddenly this was a genre that wasn't just for Koreans; the West had woken up to a new sound and a new style of performance.

WHY DO WE LOVE K-POP?

It's not just about the music, it's about the personalities, the fashion, the big-budget, visually stimulating music videos with their sleek and flawless choreography. It's also about the excitement of the modern pop, and its contemporary, catchy and upbeat sound. We love the big groups and the iconic solo stars, their individual styles and music that is constantly evolving.

Spotlight: BTS

Arguably the biggest K-pop band of the moment, BTS have been on the K-pop scene since 2013. The seven members are heavily involved in every aspect of their music, from the songwriting and production to the choreography and visual concepts; their music covers themes relevant to their Korean fanbase and they write lyrics about the difficulties of growing up, learning to love yourself and the stressful school system in Korea. They became the first K-pop group to address the United Nations due to their charity work with Unicef, as part of a campaign called Generation Unlimited, which focuses on encouraging young people to believe in their own convictions. They have previously worked with Unicef on another global initiative, #ENDviolence, by advocating their 'Love Myself' movement, building on their belief that true love first begins with loving yourself.

Opposite: PSY performs at the 2013 MuchMusic Video Awards at MuchMusic HQ, Toronto, Canada

'People say, "Don't judge a book by its cover," so why do they judge music by its language?'

Spotlight: EXO

Formed in 2011, the super popular boyband showcased their songs to a worldwide audience when they performed at the closing ceremony of the 2018 Winter Olympics in Pyeongchang. The band used to be split in half: EXO-K (who sang in Korean) and EXO-M (who sang in Mandarin); however, they now perform as one unit. They are regarded as one of the most innovative K-pop bands, with the concept that they are all aliens from EXOPLANET who have come to Earth with superpowers – references to this backstory are threaded through their music videos and performances.

Spotlight: Blackpink

The four-piece band, consisting of Jisoo, Jennie, Rosé and Lisa, is the best-known K-pop girl band outside of Korea. They were the first female K-pop band to perform at Coachella in 2019. Their world tour has seen them perform in the UK, Canada and across America and they have their own reality TV series too, *Blackpink House.*

Opposite top: EXO 'The ElyXiOn' world tour concert 2018 in Taipei, Taiwan

Opposite bottom: Blackpink perform during the 2019 Coachella Festival, California

Spotlight: TWICE

The nine-member girl band has not only attracted legions of fans in South Korea and America, they have seen unparalleled success in Japan, too, playing to crowds of 50,000 when they toured there. They have been recognized in the K-pop community as a group that isn't afraid to speak out about mental health; one of their members, Mina, didn't join the band on their 2019 world tour due to an anxiety disorder. It was a huge and celebrated step in raising awareness of mental health.

Spotlight: G-Dragon

Lead singer of K-pop hip-hop group Big Bang, G-Dragon has been dubbed 'the King of K-pop' by *Rolling Stone*, *Dazed* and *Vogue* thanks to his global influence as a singer-songwriter, rapper, entrepreneur and fashion icon. G-Dragon's popularity, style and eclectic flair has won him admiration from across the fashion world. In 2020 he finished his military service (a compulsory duty for all Korean men), but his time out of the spotlight didn't dampen his popularity; his fame is in a league of its own.

FACT

In the year of its release, 2012, the music video for PSY's 'Gangnam Style' exceeded 1 million views on YouTube, the first video to do so in the history of the website. As of 2020, it has racked up over 3 billion views.

K팝 스포트라이트

Spotlight: Holland

When Holland came out as the first openly gay K-pop idol in 2018, it shocked many in his socially conservative home country. South Korea does not legally recognize same-sex unions, and the video for his debut single, 'Neverland', which featured him kissing another man, received a 19+ age rating. But within twenty-four hours it had gained over half a million views on YouTube worldwide, making Holland an instant voice for the LGBTQ+ community in a K-pop world that hadn't seen this topic raised so openly before. His real name is Go Tae-seob, but he chose Holland as his stage name in honour of the Netherlands – the first country to legalize same-sex marriage.

DANCE LIKE A K-POP STAR

Want to perfect the iconic shuffling-crab move from the Girls' Generation 'Gee' choreography? Or the finger-snapping of Super Junior's 'Sorry Sorry'? Learning the jaw-dropping dance routines of your favourite K-pop stars has never been easier; it's pretty common for K-pop groups to upload 'dance practice' videos to YouTube, where you get to see them performing the full choreography in a dance studio, without any of the cutaways and crazy camera angles of the ultra-slick music videos. There are also plenty of fan-made step-by-step choreography tutorials available online, so there is no excuse for you not to learn your favourite dance moves from the comfort of your own home.

THE ULTIMATE K-POP PLAYLIST

'GANGNAM STYLE' **PSY**

'COME BACK HOME'
SEO TAIJI AND BOYS

'CANDY' **H.O.T.**

'COUPLE' **SECHSKIES**

'MINISKIRT' **AOA**

'ROCKING' **TEEN TOP**

'GEE' **GIRLS' GENERATION**

'LUCIFER' **SHINEE**

'HANDS UP' **2PM**

'ABRACADABRA'
BROWN EYED GIRLS

'MIROTIC' **TVXQ!**

'CATALLENA'
ORANGE CARAMEL

'SORRY SORRY' **SUPER JUNIOR**

'TOUCH MY BODY' **SISTAR**

'BAD' **INFINITE**

'MR.' **KARA**

'IT'S RAINING' **RAIN**

'SO HOT' **WONDER GIRLS**

'I AM THE BEST' **2NE1**

'PERFECT MAN' **SHINHWA**

'ELECTRIC SHOCK' **F(X)**

'HER' **BLOCK B**

'FXXK IT' **BIGBANG**

'VOODOO DOLL' **VIXX**

'UP & DOWN' **EXID**

'BLOOD SWEAT & TEARS' **BTS**

'MONSTER' **EXO**

'HARD CARRY' **GOT7**

'HERO' **MONSTA X**

'ALL I WANNA DO' **JAY PARK**

'CLAP' **SEVENTEEN**

'HIP' **MAMAMOO**

'NEVERLAND' **HOLLAND**

'FANCY' **TWICE**

'CROWN' **TXT**

'BAD BOY' **RED VELVET**

'MY PACE' **STRAY KIDS**

'THE 7TH SENSE' **NCT U**

'SNAPPING' **CHUNGHA**

'SAY MY NAME' **ATEEZ**

'NOIR' **SUNMI**

'KICK IT' **NCT 127**

'DDU-DU DDU-DU' **BLACKPINK**

K-POP NOT YOUR THING?

If you like alternative hip-hop: Epik High is a hip-hop trio who have been releasing music since 2001. They played Coachella in 2016 and have a large global fanbase thanks to their slick beats and thoughtful lyrics.

If you like R&B: Hoody made her debut in 2013 and was the first female vocalist to sign to record label AOMG. She has collaborated with the likes of ELO, Cokejazz and Jay Park.

If you like electronic indie rock: The Solutions originally debuted as a duet before two more members joined in 2014. Despite being native Korean-speakers, they often perform songs in English – nineties British pop is a heavy influence – on worldwide tours of Asia, Europe and America.

If you like punk: Crying Nut have been on the punk scene since 1995 and are known as the godfathers of Korean punk. They recorded the official Team Korea song for the 2002 FIFA World Cup.

If you like indie folk: OKDAL are a female duo, also known as Rooftop Moonlight, who attract fans who like their lyrics full of wisdom and straight-talking.

If you like soulful pop: Singer-songwriter IU is known as a 'vocal queen' and has not only written and produced songs for several TV and film soundtracks, she has also collaborated with some of the biggest names in K-pop, like PSY and G-Dragon.

If you like rap: Singer, songwriter, rapper, solo artist and boyband member (as the lead singer of Block B), the multitalented Zico is a respected hip-hop artist as well as an idol, with a wide and varied discography of catchy hits.

한국 스타일

k-dramas

What to binge-watch, what to avoid and how to bring the most talked about Korean films into your life

EMBRACE THE DRAMA

**'If I pause my K-drama
to reply to you,
trust me, you're special.'**

K-drama isn't a guilty pleasure, it's an art form and it's addictive like no other TV you have ever watched. And don't be misled by the name – the drama in K-drama comes from the Korean word deurama, which just means any scripted television show. K-dramas cover the whole spectrum: romance to sci-fi, police procedural to period drama, comedy to thriller, and political satire to medical drama.

WHEN K-DRAMA BECAME COOL

The back catalogue for K-drama is extensive; they've been broadcast since the 1960s, but it was only in the mid-1990s that they started to get really popular, when there was a shift in style, production and plot. This started happening when slick, big-budget American TV shows began streaming into Korean homes; it was time for Korean TV to show the world that they could produce the same addictive, popular and conversation-starting programmes, so they upped their game. Money was poured into the K-drama industry and the genre, which might have once relied on over-the-top melodrama, now had cash to spend on production values instead.

City Hall might seem dated by today's standards, but when it aired in 2009 it was a fresh, good-guy-wins political drama – with a hefty dose of romance thrown in, of course. *Vampire Prosecutor*, which aired in 2011, is also worth a watch, especially if you liked the US series *Dexter*. Protagonist Min Tae-yeon is a criminal investigator who, having been bitten by a vampire, can see a victim's final moments by tasting their blood. The themes, dialogue and plot can be a bit cheesy, but it represents a shift in style for Korean TV, and the modern K-drama was born.

FACT

Kingdom was the first K-drama to stream its first series on Netflix (without being broadcast on television first), and its popularity has paved the way for other original Korean series to premiere on the platform. The hotly anticipated second series is now also available.

K-DRAMA STRUCTURE

Here's a overview of how K-drama series work:

Seasons are usually between sixteen and twenty-four episodes long (although *Queen Seondeok* was originally planned for a shorter run but lasted for a blockbusting sixty-two episodes).

○

Each episode is normally sixty minutes long, though some final episodes may be nearer to ninety minutes.

○

The epic length of the seasons means that only a handful of the most popular shows get renewed for a second season.

○

Because there is often only one season, the final episode never leaves the audience on a cliffhanger or with loose ends to tie up.

○

No shows are cancelled or shortened in the series; you won't feel short-changed.

Top left: Actor Yum Jung-ah attends the 51st Baeksang Arts Awards in Seoul, South Korea, 2015

Top right: Actor Lee Jong-suk attends the photocall for Alexander McQueen 2018

Right: The statue on Nami Island, South Korea, pays tribute to the series *Winter Sonata*

Having a famous face in a K-drama can help to make it a success before it has even aired. A show will quite often centre the publicity around its main star because they know their fans will get heavily involved in the show.

O

K-dramas are big-budget, high-production affairs with lots filmed on location in other countries and featuring cutting-edge special effects.

TOP 10 K-DRAMAS TO WATCH, BY GENRE:

Like romance? If you thought that having an office romance was a big no-no, this down-to-earth love story might change your mind. *Romance Is a Bonus Book* is about two people working at a publishing agency whose relationship blossoms as the series develops.

Like action? *Vagabond* stars leading actor Lee Seung-gi as a stuntman who finds himself in a web of corruption as he searches for the truth behind a plane crash that killed his nephew. Basically, this ticks all the spy/action/thriller boxes.

Like political dramas? If you liked *House of Cards*, chances are you will like *Chief of Staff*. An ambitious employee tries to make his way to the top by outwitting anyone who gets in his way.

Like sci-fi? *Memories of the Alhambra* will win you over if you like your TV shows packed with sci-fi slickness. Videogame designer Jung Se-joo creates an alternative reality where users can find weapons to use in the real world.

Like star-crossed lovers? *Crash Landing on You* follows a South Korean woman whose paragliding trip is blown off course by a tornado – she ends up in North Korea, falling for the elite North Korean Special Police Force Captain who found her.

Like costume dramas? *Queen Seondeok* may have first aired in 2009 but this biopic based on the life of Queen Seondeok of Silla is one of the best-regarded K-dramas of all time. Queen Seondeok has to prove she has what it takes to rule the kingdom when others make a bid for the throne.

Like drama dramas? At fifty-two episodes long, *The Last Empress* is not for the faint-hearted and will require a lot of concentration as the plot is very involved. Set in an alternate universe, South Korea is under the rule of a royal family with its fair share of secrets.

Like big hitters? Featuring one of Korea's leading actresses, Bae Doona, the *Stranger* series was bought by Netflix for over £150,000 per episode when it first aired. With the *New York Times* rating it one of the best shows of 2017, it's no wonder there is a lot of excitement surrounding the second series.

Like medical drama? *Good Doctor* only ran for twenty episodes but was so popular it sparked an American version called *The Good Doctor* with Freddie Highmore in the lead role. The drama focuses on an autistic doctor proving his worth in the fiercely competitive world of paediatric surgery.

Like a little bit of everything? *Kingdom* doesn't fit neatly into one genre as the story revolves around Crown Prince Chang trying to eliminate an influx of zombies. Think supernatural historical thriller with so much more.

자격 있는 오스카 수상작

OSCAR-WORTHY WINNER

When Bong Joon-ho's *Parasite* scooped the Best Picture award at the 2020 Academy Awards, it marked a huge turning point for Korean cinema. Never before had a Korean film made such an impact in Hollywood. *Parasite* was the first non-English language film to win the coveted award in the ninety-two-year history of the Oscars.

Part black comedy, part thriller, part scathing social commentary about class and money, *Parasite* sees the poor Kim family infiltrate the huge house of the wealthy Park family, before things turn very dark.

The buzz surrounding the film started at the Cannes Film Festival. It then scooped a Golden Globe Award for Best Foreign Language Film and a BAFTA for Best Film Not in the English Language. At the Oscars it was triumphant, winning not only Best Picture but also Best Director, Best Original Screenplay and Best International Feature Film.

MOVIE MAGIC: KOREAN-STYLE

If films like *Parasite* have ignited a love of Korean drama on the big screen, here are three other Korean films (available with subtitles) that run on a similar psychological theme:

The Spy Gone North, released in 2018, is a tense thriller based on the true story of Park Chae-seo, a South Korean operative who became famous under his codename, Black Venus.

For an older cult flick, look no further than the 2006 blockbuster **The Host**, also directed by Bong Joon-ho. This tells the story of a monstrous amphibian created when a US military pathologist disposes of large quantities of formaldehyde down a drain in Seoul, polluting the Han River where the monster is formed.

Train to Busan is an equally popular film and a masterpiece in the zombie genre. It was so popular when it hit the big screen in 2016 that it has sparked a sequel, as well as plans for an English-language remake. The plot revolves around a father and daughter and their fellow passengers on a train bound for Busan, while a zombie outbreak tears through the country. The suspense and intensity build as the passengers realize their fellow commuters might well be infected.

The classic, award-winning film **The Way Home** is also worth a mention because it's the complete opposite of *Train to Busan*. Released in 2002, this heartfelt tale of sentiment sees a young boy full of attitude sent to live with his very old and mute grandmother. And there's not a zombie in sight.

CHAPTER ⑤

한국스타의

korean
food

Happy eating: bringing Korean cuisine into your home

KOREAN FOOD: HEALTHY FOOD, HEALTHY YOU

'If it doesn't nourish your skin or your soul, don't eat it.'

It's simple to understand that the holistic approach to Korean beauty starts with the food you eat: what you put in your body will have a direct effect on your skin, hair, nails and mood. To look your best, you must feel your best and that's why we need the proper nutrients in our body to make this happen. Korean food is generally a mixture of grilled meats and fish, lots of steamed and fermented vegetables and, of course, a healthy serving of rice which is a staple of Korean cuisine.

Food is at the heart of how people socialize, and the phrase 'Bap meogeosseoyo?' which translates to 'Have you eaten?' is a common Korean greeting.

KOREAN SUPERFOODS

Kimchi

This spicy cabbage dish is one of the most popular foods in Korea, and it's served with pretty much every meal (see *Top 5 Korean foods to try* on p104). The reason it is so good for you is because it's fermented. Fermentation produces a variety of living micro-organisms which can help fight off harmful bacteria in your gut and improve your digestion. Kimchi can also help regulate cholesterol and boost your immune system, and is a good source of vitamins A, B and C.

Seaweed

Seaweed takes many guises in Korean cuisine, but it doesn't matter how you eat it (as a soup, to wrap rice or meat, etc.), it's beneficial for your body in all its forms because of the vitamins and minerals it contains. In Korea, it is traditional to eat a seaweed soup called miyeok-guk on your birthday; this soup is also given to new mothers after childbirth because of its high levels of iron.

Opposite: (top) Bibimbap, (bottom right) dalgona
coffee, (bottom far right) bulgogi beef slices fried
with sesame and carrot

Doenjang

This fermented, slightly salty soybean paste is a great source
of protein and is the main ingredient in doenjang jiggae, a stew
that is also rich in collagen – good for smooth and healthy skin.
Doenjang also contains linolenic acid, which can help prevent
cholesterol plaques building up in your arteries and helps with
blood circulation.

Gochujang

Found in many Korean dishes, such as bibimbap (rice with a variety
of vegetables and often meat and egg) and bibimguksu (the same,
but with noodles), this fiery fermented paste made from chilli
peppers and soybeans aids digestion so that your skin can absorb
the vital nutrients it needs to thrive. Gochujang also promotes
blood circulation and is thought to help prevent blood clots.

Skin-boosting broths

Collagen is responsible for healthy, firm complexions that retain
moisture, but the supply your body makes of this wonder protein
depletes over the years. This might be why Koreans make sure
that food that is rich in collagen is such a staple part of their
diet. It is found in the bones and skin of animals, so fish is often
roasted skin-on, while stews and broths are full of collagen
because they are made from a bone broth (whether its chicken,
beef or fish).

TEA-TIME BENEFITS

Tea is a popular drink in Korea, and while the exhaustive benefits of different herbal teas are well documented, these favourite Korean cuppas are worth a specific mention.

Barley tea: This caffeine-free drink is made by brewing roasted barley seeds and is often drunk after a meal. The tea is an amazing digestive aid and potent antioxidant too; some scientific studies suggest it is also a good anticoagulant, or blood thinner, that helps keep your heart and vital organs functioning well. It also helps bring down a temperature, so Korean parents will often encourage their children to drink it if they have a fever.

o

Green tea: Green tea is such a popular staple drink and ingredient in the skin-conscious world of K-beauty that one of the country's largest beauty brands,

AmorePacific, has its own green tea plantation. Rich in antioxidants, green tea is believed to be particularly beneficial for oily or acne-prone skin.

○

Yulmu-cha: This distinctly nutty-flavoured, high protein tea is made from the seeds of the yulmu plant, which are roasted, ground into powder and then dissolved in warm water.

○

Ginseng: Made from the root of the ginseng plant, this popular drink is often used as an anti-anxiety beverage thanks to its ability to regulate the body's response to stress.

○

Korean persimmon punch (sujeonggwa): This is a popular traditional dessert drink which can be enjoyed hot or cold and is made from water, dried persimmon and cinnamon. It is dark brown and full of vibrant sweet and spicy aromas and is especially good after a large meal as it aids digestion.

○

Yuja-cha: Mostly drunk in the winter, this citrus infusion is prepared by marinating sliced yuja (otherwise known as yuzu, a lemon-like citrus fruit) with sugar or honey and then leaving it for a couple of days. Then, add hot water to create a sweet and sour tea that contains flavonoids and limonoids which are thought to help prevent serious illnesses.

○

Corn tea: You can either make this with dried silk corn to produce a lightly roasted flavour or use roasted corn kernels, which produce a deeper flavour. Or better yet, use a combination! Corn tea is good for overcoming fatigue.

Omija tea: Omija means 'five berry' and you can taste the five different flavours (sweet, sour, salty, bitter and spicy) in this one berry. It is good for tickly coughs. Not just your average cuppa!

○

Bubble tea: Bubble tea, or boba tea, is made from tea, milk, ice, syrup and chewy tapioca pearls. There are many flavour variations – one of the most famous is milk tea with black sugar pearls, called black sugar bubble tea.

KOREAN COFFEE – ICE, ICE BABY!

Coffee is a big deal in Korea; you'll see people drinking it out and about pretty much everywhere. One of the most popular forms is iced coffee, which comes in many varieties.

TABLE MANNERS AND TIME

Korean dining is an important part of the day and it is a communal and sociable affair. 'Jalmeokgesseumnida' ('I will eat well') is a compliment that is said before the meal, reaffirming your belief that what you are about to put in your body will only benefit it. It is also a traditional word to say to a host if you are eating with another family – a polite signal that you are grateful and looking forward to the meal you are about to eat.

'Cooking a nutritious meal
is one of the great gifts you can
give to those you love.'

DINE IN KOREAN STYLE:
BONDING OVER FOOD

Rather than everyone having their own individual portion, Korean cuisine is based around small bowls and lots of side dishes, as the idea is to share out everything you eat. Mealtimes are a communal, relaxed and sociable event, with several 'main' dishes and a variety of banchan (side dishes like kimchi, beansprouts and seasoned spinach – it's not truly a Korean meal without banchan) enjoyed together with good conversation. You could opt for a plate of meat in the middle of your table which can either be cooked as the other food is eaten (the ritual of cooking over a small stove is shared among all the guests) or pre-grill a plate of meat so it can come straight out as a centrepiece.

It's also worth mentioning how certain types of alcoholic and non-alcoholic beverages are consumed and play a part in the sociable dining experience too. The most popular alcoholic drink is soju, the Korean national liquor, which is a clear, slightly sweet-tasting spirit. Look out for certain foods involving the word anju, which means food that is specifically made to be eaten with alcohol. As a general rule, when you are dining, the oldest person around the table fills up the shot glasses with soju when you first

길거리 음식

start. After that, you don't ever pour your own drink; you fill up your neighbour's glass before waiting for them to fill up yours. This is to encourage a sense of bonding and solidarity as you eat and drink together.

Opposite: (top) tteokbokki, (centre right) hotteok, (bottom) pajeon

STREET FOOD

Street food is at the heart of Korean food culture and the popularity of street-food vendors means you are never far from a delicious, quickly prepared and expertly cooked snack. The smells and the colours of the food are irresistible, as vendors mix and cook with the spices and sauces, and the food they are preparing in front of you becomes a delicious form of entertainment.

But if you don't like the idea of eating as you stroll down a pavement or weave in and out of a steady stream of commuters, you can always try the most popular types of street food, like tteokbokki, hotteok or pajeon, in the comfort of your own home instead. Tteokbokki, one of the most popular street-food snacks, is chewy, cylindrical rice cakes cooked with gochujang. Hotteok is a pancake-style snack with a sweet filling and is particularly popular in the winter months. If you don't have a sweet tooth, opt for a more savoury filling – cheese or kimchi are favourite alternatives. Another quick and simple street-food snack is

pajeon, in which batter is poured over green onions in a hot pan. These versatile dishes are great to experiment with too – use leftovers in your fridge for a more personalized jeon.

KOREAN BBQS:
SIZZLING MEAT AND MEMORABLE MEALS

A Korean BBQ is not the same sort of occasion as a Western-style BBQ. There is no outdoor grill brought out in the hot summer months and no self-appointed chef with a set of tongs – a Korean BBQ is served inside and throughout the year. Traditionally, this type of meal simply refers to the communal activity of cooking raw meat. A grill takes centre stage on your dining table and, once it's hot, you simply add thin slices of pork, chicken and beef which have been marinated in all manner of spicy sauces. Small side dishes full of lettuce, garlic, peppers and chilli pastes fill up the rest of the table for you to make meat wraps.

BBQ delights include samgyeopsal, a popular dish that consists of grilled slices of pork belly meat which is then dipped in a salt and pepper seasoning, wrapped in lettuce with grilled slices of onion and garlic, shredded green onions and kimchi.

Bulgogi is strips of beef (or opt for pork or chicken strips if you prefer) that is marinated in a sweet soy sauce with lots of garlic and sesame oil before being cooked and eaten with grilled onions and rice, with lettuce or other leafy vegetables used to wrap it up. You can do a similar thing with aubergine, if you're a vegetarian.

Galbi, which means 'rib', is simply a good-sized slab of meat that is marinated in soy sauce, chopped garlic and sugar before being grilled.

TOP 5 KOREAN FOODS TO TRY

1 **Kimchi.** A vital part of every Korean meal, this food dates back at least 2,000 years, and is made by fermenting cabbage with seasonings including Korean chilli flakes, garlic, green onions and shrimp. There are over a hundred different kinds of kimchi and it's a Korean essential.

TRY: Kimchi fried rice is a great introduction to kimchi, as the cooking process mellows out the flavours a little. Or, if you're not keen on cabbage, why not try radish kimchi?

2 **Japchae.** This is a popular dish and one that is quick and easy to rustle up at home. You start with sweet potato starch noodles and mix any combination of vegetables you have to hand, such as mushrooms, green onions, carrots and spinach, as well as long strips of beef or pork into a sesame oil and soy sauce mixture.

TRY: If you don't eat meat, why not substitute it with some extra shiitake mushrooms, or try a spicy seafood variation instead.

3 **Bibimbap.** Mix together rice, vegetables, beef and egg with gochujang and sesame oil. This is a perfect meal for when you want a hearty yet quick-to-prepare dish.

TRY: This versatile dish means you can use up any combination of vegetables or meat you have left over from other meals. Bacon and fried egg bibimbap (swapping the beef for bacon and frying an egg instead of having it raw) is a popular alternative.

4 **Tteokguk.** Add oval rice cake slices and egg to a meat-based broth (usually beef) and let the hearty warmth of the dish fill your soul. This was traditionally eaten on the first day of the Korean new year, but its popularity means the soup is now eaten all year round.

TRY: Add some flavoursome kimchi mandu (dumplings) to complement the mild flavours of the broth.

5 **Korean BBQ.** Cook your raw meat on the grill before wrapping it in lettuce and kimchi and then dip it in some spicy dipping sauce. There are two popular sauces to try: ssamjang, which is made with gochujang and doenjang and a few extras, or saeujeot, a pink-coloured salty sauce made with tiny fermented shrimp.

TRY: Bossam, a simple yet delicious pork dish where the cuts of meat are boiled rather than barbecued before being dipped in sauce.

COOKING KOREAN STYLE

Korean Bapsang (www.koreanbapsang.com), **Maangchi** (www.maangchi.com) and **My Korean Kitchen** (www.mykoreankitchen.com) are just a few websites that offer some amazing recipes ideas for cooking up Korean food in your home.

한국 스타일

simple home

How to bring Korean lifestyle influences into your home and adopt a sense of calm and well-being

CLUTTER SMOTHERS, SIMPLICITY BREATHES:
THE EMOTIONS OF YOUR ENVIRONMENT

'Surround yourself with things that you love, that are authentic to you and your home becomes your story.'

There are no set rules when it comes to creating your perfect bedroom or living space – other than that it should be a reflection of who you are and what you love. It should be a sanctuary, an expression of your passions, and it should give an insight into your world, your inner self and reveal your curiosities.

It is widely accepted that keeping your bedroom clear of clutter and mess helps create a calm environment, and minimalist interiors make it so much easier to find serenity.

집에서의
평온함과
행복

Modern Korean interior design celebrates:

○ Functional comfort and elegant simplicity

○ Creative vibes and soothing touches

○ Traditional Korean aesthetics and
   contemporary design

○ Playful textures and soft colourful tones

Fill your bedroom with calm

A bedroom should be a place of rest and peace and therefore it is considered best to keep it minimal. But that doesn't mean sparse or boring. The idea is to keep mess and clutter to a minimum to allow your room to be filled with your energy.

Making the bed neat and comfortable is the key to getting that Korean vibe. Koreans like a practical but stylish bed and prefer 100 per cent cotton or smooth-textured bedding. Simple and stylish patterns and colours are popular, and a small but functional bedside table is considered a necessity.

Don't think that you should limit yourself to just the bare basics – accessories like throws, rugs, cushions and blankets play a key part in creating comfort and style.
(see *Accessories* on p121)

Try to remember that what you have in your room should represent what you value in your life. Nothing should be in there just because you think you should have it.

○

Never underestimate the power of letting go of things that no longer have a purpose in your life. In the same way you would throw out old beauty products and make-up that is out of date, taking the time to assess your bedroom and re-evaluate how much you thrive living among all your belongings is very therapeutic. If you haven't worn that T-shirt in three years, get rid of it!

○

Don't let your 'stuff' be 'stifling'. If the thought of getting rid of something isn't appealing and yet you want to organize it better, opt for sleek storage instead. You still have what you want around you but out of sight and tidied away.

K-POP INFLUENCES

Are you a K-pop fanatic? Here's how to organize your stuff. If the rest of your room is chilled and calm you will be able to make your K-pop shelf – with keepsakes, merchandise and albums – a focal point. Have a look on Pinterest and YouTube for inspiration on how to create and maintain your own K-pop shelf and tutorials on how to reorganize 'ugly' shelves to help motivate you.

K-pop shelf dos and don'ts

Do try to get a shelving unit rather than one
simple shelf. You'll be able to fit in lots more.

O

Don't worry about getting a super aesthetically pleasing
shelf; the stuff on it should be displayed with care
and be the stylish bit, not the shelf itself.

O

Do try to keep to a colour scheme if possible as visually
this looks more beautiful. (You could use the official
colour of your favourite K-pop band or artist as the
theme for your shelf.)

O

Do keep mementoes that are valuable in pretty boxes
or frames to protect them that little bit more.

O

Don't worry about trying to fill a shelf for the sake of it;
if you don't have much to start with, make the most of
what you do have by setting it in the centre and let your
collection grow around it.

O

Do remember that the keepsakes on your shelf
are all personal preference – your loves and your
memories only.

간단하고 소박한

LOOKING FOR SIMPLICITY?

1 Focus on one area of a room to begin with. Maybe your workspace or wardrobe should be your starting point? If it's just untidy it won't take long, but if it needs to be cleared once and for all then allow yourself a bit more time.

2 Ask a friend to come into your room and tell you what the first thing is that their eyes are drawn to. If they say a messy bookcase or overflowing cupboard, that would be a good starting point.

3 When you are deciding on whether to keep or throw away, ask yourself whether you have used this item in the past year. If not, there is your answer.

4 Be a ruthless editor of what you allow into your home from now on. Before you buy something, think about where it will go and what purpose it will serve.

5 Keep visualizing the space you want to be living in and take inspiration from Instagram and Pinterest. Seeing how others have worked with small spaces or used lighting is a great way to be inspired for your own room. Look for **#koreaninterior #koreaninteriortips**

Remember that organizing your space and reorganizing your home into a simple, minimalist space will reduce your stress levels. You will be able to come home to a clean, clutter-free environment that will calm rather than frazzle your senses.

'Essential oils can be your natural "go-to" source for stress relief, recuperation and mental rejuvenation.'

ANGELA AMBROSE-RADFORD

CALM AND SOOTHING: FINDING YOUR ESSENTIAL OIL

Aromatherapy oils can create an atmosphere of balance and calm, helping transform your room into a place of tranquillity. Different aromatherapy oils invoke different feelings – they can make you feel relaxed, motivated, calm or full of energy, depending on the oil you choose. They can influence your behaviour, your memory, your mood and your senses and provide a therapeutic effect on your emotions.

EMOTIONALLY BALANCED: AROMATHERAPY OILS TO HAVE AT HOME

Here are some of the different essential oils you can try, depending on how you feel. You could also mix a few drops of two or more together to create your own unique scent for your room.

If you are feeling anxious: Lavender, bergamot, frankincense, orange, peppermint, geranium, lemon, eucalyptus.

If you are feeling unbalanced: Clary sage, rose, cedarwood, geranium, jasmine, sandalwood.

If you are feeling tired: Basil, bergamot, frankincense, tea tree, lemon, peppermint, ginger.

If you are feeling unconfident: Bergamot, orange, jasmine, lemon, rosemary, grapefruit, peppermint.

If you are feeling angry: Jasmine, lavender, rose, bergamot, ylang-ylang, orange, cedarwood, camomile.

If you need clarity: Frankincense, tea tree, eucalyptus, lemon, wild orange, sandalwood.

INTERIOR IDEAS: KOREAN INSPIRATIONS

Bringing Korean influences into your home can be done with simple ideas: colour, lighting, furniture, accessories and nature. However big your room or the space you are looking to change, we have listed a range of inspiring suggestions to help you create a place of personality, wellbeing and calm.

Go for colours that are sleek, clean, crisp and fresh but never cold; the colour of your walls will be the setting for your room. If you can, use the same colour on the ceiling as your walls, as this helps smaller rooms 'stretch' by providing a visual flow to the room.

Colour choices

Opt for a **white colour palette** (this cultivates clarity, precision and communication), **light grey tones** (provides a harmonious union between black and white), **pale lemons** (a colour associated with purifying and bringing love), **green pastels** (represents growth and new beginnings) or **dusky pink tones** ('millennial pink' is a very versatile colour and works well with contrasting tones of whites, greys and blacks) – these will all provide a simple and warm welcoming vibe.

Wallpaper wonders

Stick on wallpapers and wall prints are a versatile way of adding a playful, personal stamp to a room and a great way to bring the theme of your room right on trend. There's a huge range of designs available, which means you can change the look and feel of your room with great ease – the choice is endless and the designs and colours on offer mean you are likely to find a design that works for your decor requirements. Colours, styles and patterns vary, as does the quality and durability, but these decorating adhesives are ideally suited for quick and easy transformations. Depending on the look you are going for, you can opt for plain, muted tones with added texture, ornate designs for smaller areas of wall, tile patterns, brick facades, linen, wood or marble.

Instagram and Pinterest have lots of interior design ideas using these materials so it's unlikely you will be stuck for inspiration. Low-budget and user-friendly, a lot of the stick-on wallpapers require you to do just that – peel and stick – while others might need an extra adhesive. The added appeal of these decorating delights is that you can peel them off without damaging the wall underneath, meaning it's ready for the next design of your choice. And if you are careful when you peel off, the stick-on paper can be reused for another wall. You can even find waterproof and fireproof styles, for use on kitchen walls.

TIP | If you are tight for space, adding a large framed mirror to one of your walls is a good way of reflecting light around your room, giving the illusion of a larger area.

'Take note of what light does – to everything.'

TESS GUINERY

Light

Your room should be a celebration of natural light and the most effective way to do this is to let light in by removing heavy, thick, dark curtains and replacing them with lighter and more see-through materials. The artificial lighting you have in your room is generally split into three areas: main lighting, task lighting and accent lighting.

Your main light is the actual 'whole' lighting of the room; the functional light you switch on when you come into a room. Even coverage of the light is good to project a feeling of 'balance' when you enter a room.

Task lighting is specific to a certain area, like a desk or make-up table. This light is more focused on the enhancement of a particular spot. Moveable and bright, these lights are often versatile lamps that can be used as a spotlight.

Accent lighting brings a sense of warmth and 'glow' to a room. They can add an element of cosiness to a space that might benefit from a personal touch, like the use of fairy lights over a picture board or a couple of softer illuminating wall lights over a bed.

Furniture

How does the room make you feel and what is the room's purpose? There are some key changes you can make with your furniture choices which will help shape your home into a Korean-inspired

한국적인
분위기

place of tranquillity. A calm, zen-like space is exactly what Asian decor embodies. Utilizing space efficiently is key, so that even if your home isn't the most spacious, it will still feel open and liveable.

For example, in a bedroom, your bed is your main item of furniture, so try to choose low and unfussy bed frames in wood rather than metal. Light-coloured wood surrounds are ideal or, if not, keep the headboards or footboards low or remove them.

Accessories

When it comes to accessories, eclectic is quite often the key to a stylish Korean-influenced home. The rest of your room might be a sea of calm but your accessories speak volumes about you and your personality. This doesn't mean that the 'extras' in a room are loud and seem out of place – the accessories you choose are simply an extension of who you are. Mix old and new pieces, traditional and quaint, cheap and expensive, handmade and luxurious – the choice is yours.

Cushions, rugs and throws can all work to bring a pop of colour to neutrally toned rooms. The range and style is a personal choice, but don't be afraid of mixing different styles and fabrics. For example, a plain-coloured, thick-piled rug can be complemented by cushions in bold, quirky prints. Or a luxurious, elegant-looking throw can sit against a row of quilted, tasselled, pom-pom-adorned or fringed cushions.

Browse Instagram, Pinterest or Etsy to be inspired by artists and designs that complement the colour schemes in your room. Framed typography prints are a beautiful way of reminding yourself of lifestyle mantras you want to bring into your life, or simple, sketched artwork can be equally as powerful.

If your room is all about displaying K-pop posters and artwork, try putting them in sleek frames of complementary sizes. Why not arrange your plentiful K-pop photos around a larger poster and make it a focal point? Or, if you are going for single framed photos of each of the members of BTS, for example, line up all seven in complementary frames and position them in an artistic, abstract way on a feature wall.

BEAUTIFUL BOTANICALS

Become inspired by the outdoors and bring that into your home by adding a houseplant to your room. Not only will the plant add a striking splash of green (the colour of energy, harmony, safety and tranquillity), you'll be making a connection to nature and its harmonies.

The Korean lifestyle emphasizes self-care and wellness and below are some of the most popular houseplants to embrace for their physical and mental health benefits. Social media is filled with interior plant fans. Follow some of the most prolific Instagram influencers and bloggers who love their greenery and swap tips and advice about your own plants.

Swiss cheese plant (*Monstera deliciosa*): This is one of the most popular houseplants to have in your home thanks to it being a super-easy house guest. They don't require a lot of upkeep and their large, structural leaves make a beautiful impact in any room.

Peace lily (*Spathiphyllum*): Elegant and poised, the peace lily will bring your home exactly what it says – peace and tranquillity.

Jasmine (*Jasminum*): It's not unusual for Korean women to add jasmine flowers to their hair and your room will be filled with its charming fragrance.

Aloe vera (*Aloe vera*): Known for its soothing skin relief properties, an aloe plant is also the perfect plant to have in the bedroom because it produces oxygen at night (most plants do this during the day) and will aid in a restful night's sleep.

Moth orchid (*Phalaenopsis*): It is said in Korea that the presence of an orchid in the home can be a calming influence on everyone who lives there, reducing the levels of stress and increasing healing.

Arrowhead vine (*Syngonium podophyllum*): If you think less 'arrow' shape and more 'heart' shape, this vine is the perfect addition to any bedroom.

Fiddle leaf fig (*Ficus lyrata*): This is a popular ornamental tree and will add a striking focal point to any room.

아름다운 식물

Stylish succulents

These stylish, inexpensive plants are ideal for those wanting to bring a dash of greenery into the corner of a room and are very easy to care for. There are lots of varieties on offer so why not mix and match a trio in a neat wooden tray or display them in cute white pots on a shelf or windowsill. Some of our favourites are: string of hearts (*Ceropegia woodii*); panda plant (*Kalanchoe tomentosa*); zebra plant (*Haworthia fasciata*); echeveria (all varieties); donkey tail (*Sedum morganianum*); and saguaro cactus.

'Succulents show us that we grow stronger, more interesting and resilient not in spite of challenges but thanks to them.'

KENDRA GOHEEN

TIP

If you don't want a ready-made plant, why not buy a mix of cacti and succulent plant seeds and start from scratch? Make sure you follow the instructions on the packet and watch your colourful and unique collection grow in your favourite dish or planter.

index

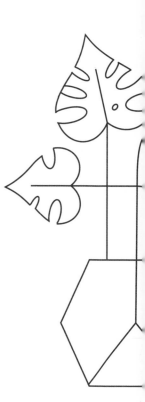

Additional illustration: Shutterstock and iStock

credits